A New True Book

ASIA

By D.V. Georges

CHILDRENS PRESS ®

CHICAGO

Hall of Supreme Harmony in the
Forbidden City, Peking, China

Library of Congress Cataloging-in-Publication Data

Georges, D. V.
    Asia.

    (A New true book)
    Includes index.
    Summary: Identifies the continent of Asia, divides
it into seven regions, including the Middle East,
Siberia, Far East, and Himalayas, and discusses their
countries, cities, and geographical features.
    1. Asia—description and travel—1951-   —Juvenile
literature. [1. Asia—Description and travel]
I. Title.
DS10.G42 1986   950   86-9631
ISBN 0-516-01288-6

PHOTO CREDITS
© Jerome Wyckoff—2

Tom Stack & Associates:
© Mickey Gibson—9 (left)
© Dominque Braud—16 (left)
© S. Chester—20 (right)
© Spencer Swanger—25 (right)
© Sheryl S. McNee—35 (left)
© Robert C. Simpson—35 (right)

Photri—10, 20 (left), 23 (right), 36 (right)

© Cameramann International, Ltd.—11, 28
(right), 40 (2 photos)

© Joan Dunlop—12 (right)

Journalism Services:
© Gregory Murphey—15, 16 (right)
© John M. Nallon—28 (left)

Valan Photos:
© Kennon Cooke—17
© B. Templeman—23 (left)
© K Ghani—29 (left)

Sovfoto—21 (left)

Root Resources:
© Irene Hubbell—21 (right)
© Byron Crader—29 (right)

© H. Armstrong Roberts—Cover, 24, 30
(left), 37, 42

Bruce Coleman Incorporated:
© H. Reinhard—25 (left)

Odyssey Productions:
© Robert Frerck—30 (right), 31 (left), 39,
41 (2 photos), 43 (left)

© H. Armstrong Roberts/Camerique—33

Al Magnus—maps 4, 7, 9, 12, 13, 19, 22,
26, 31, 32, 36, 38, 43, 45

TABLE OF CONTENTS

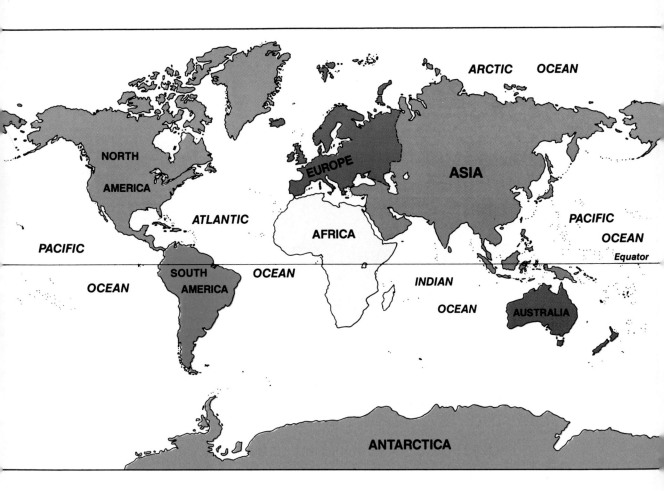

ARCTIC   OCEAN

NORTH
AMERICA

EUROPE   ASIA

ATLANTIC   PACIFIC
OCEAN
PACIFIC   AFRICA   Equator
OCEAN   SOUTH   OCEAN   INDIAN
AMERICA
OCEAN   AUSTRALIA

ANTARCTICA

FINDING ASIA

A continent is a very large mass of land. The seven continents of the world are North America, South America, Europe, Africa, Australia, Antarctica, and Asia.

The largest continent is Asia. It is the size of North America and South America together.

The Arctic, Pacific, and Indian oceans border the three coasts of Asia.

However, in western Asia, the Ural Mountains form much of the border between Europe and Asia.

The Ural Mountains are in Russia. Thus, the west part of Russia is in Europe. The east part is in Asia.

South of the Ural Mountains, the border between Asia and Europe crosses through the Caspian Sea, the Caucasus Mountains, the Black Sea, and Turkey.

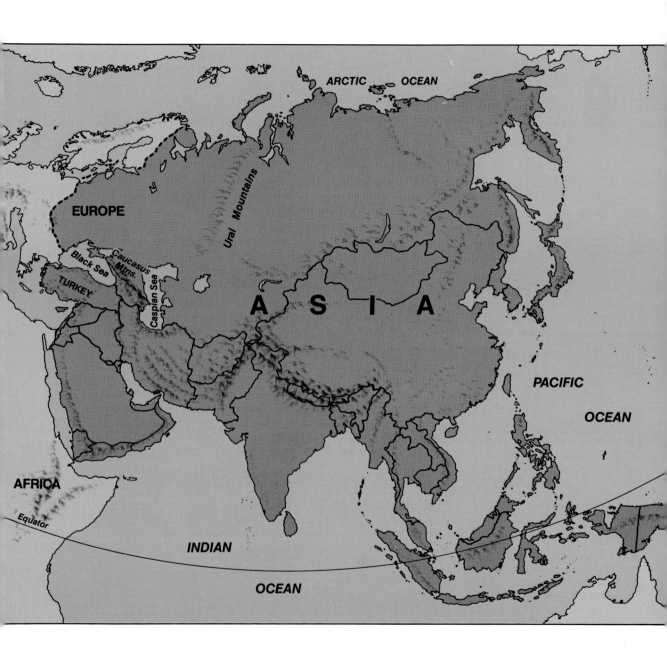

ARCTIC   OCEAN

EUROPE

Ural Mountains

Black Sea

Caucasus Mtns.

TURKEY

Caspian Sea

A S I A

PACIFIC

OCEAN

AFRICA

Equator

INDIAN

OCEAN

THE MIDDLE EAST

The countries people call the Middle East are in southwestern Asia and North Africa.

Saudi Arabia is one of the largest countries in the Middle East. It is on the Arabian Peninsula. (A peninsula is land that has water on three sides.)

The Arabian Peninsula is

between Africa and the main part of Asia. Much of the Arabian Peninsula is a sandy desert called the Arabian Desert. Under this desert, the earth is rich in oil.

Oil rig in Umm al Quiwain, United Arab Emirates

Mecca is in Saudi Arabia.

Most of the people in the Middle East are Arab Muslims. Muslims believe in a religion called Islam. Mecca is a great holy city for Muslims. It is in the southwest part of Saudi Arabia, near the Red Sea. People who are not

Jerusalem is in Israel. This is a view of the city from Mount of Olives looking to the Temple Mount with the Dome of the Rock.

Muslims cannot enter Mecca.

The Middle East is the holy land for two other important religions— Christianity, the religion of Christians, and Judaism, the religion of Jews.

Today, historic Jerusalem

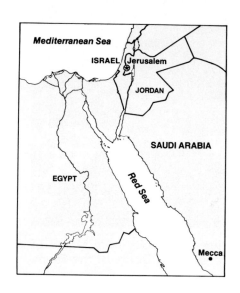

Narrow, winding streets are common in the old sections of Jerusalem.

is the capital of Israel. Scientists dig in the earth near Jerusalem. They uncover ancient scrolls and buildings. Many are thousands of years old.

12

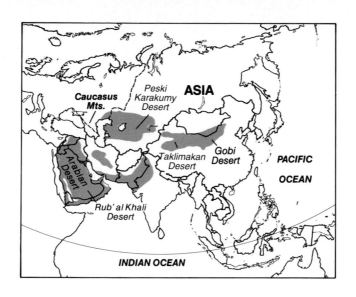

DESERTS OF ASIA

The Gobi Desert is in Mongolia and northern China. The Arabian Desert and the Gobi Desert are the two most famous deserts of Asia.

However, there are many other deserts between the

Gobi and Arabian deserts. In fact, deserts cover one fourth of Asia.

In the deserts, little rain falls and few plants grow. Where water springs up from underground, an oasis forms. Trees grow on the oasis.

Many people who live in the deserts are nomads. Nomads travel with their herds from one grassy place to another. Often,

Nomads roam the deserts.

nomads move as many as ten times in a year.

Nomads of the Gobi Desert raise sheep, goats, and cattle. In the Arabian Desert, nomads also raise Arabian camels.

The Arabian camel has one hump. Its relative, the

The Arabian, or dromedary, camel (above) and the Bactrian camel (left)

Bactrian camel, has two humps. The Bactrian camel lives in Mongolia and northern China.

Camels can go for days without water. For protection from sandy winds, camels

have two rows of thick
eyelashes. Also, their flexible
nostrils clamp shut.

Between the Caspian
Sea and the Gobi Desert
are two important deserts.
The Taklimakan Desert
is almost completely

covered with sand. It is in northwest China. Hardly anyone lives in the Taklimakan—there is not even one oasis.

More people live in the Peski Karakumy Desert, to the west. It is in southwest Turkmenistan. Part of the Peski Karakumy Desert is sandy and barren. But another part has five cities, each built around a large oasis.

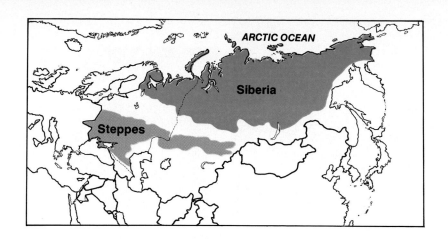

SIBERIA

Siberia is a huge part of Russia. It covers one third of Asia!

Siberia begins east of the Ural Mountains and stretches three thousand miles across Asia. Although Siberia is as large as the United States, few people live there.

Church (left) and farm (right) near Irkutsk, Siberia

In the north, Siberia borders the Arctic Ocean. Winters there last nine months!

In southern Siberia, the plains are called steppes. Little rain falls and few trees grow on the steppes.

An open cut coal mine (left) in the Chita region of Siberia and the railroad station of the Trans-Siberian line in Irkutsk (right)

Between north and south, a great forest grows. Most people in Siberia live in this central region. They work on farms or in the timber trade. Also, they work in the large coal mines and oil fields of Siberia.

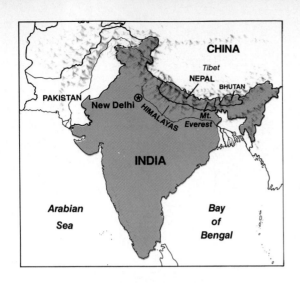

THE HIMALAYAS

The Himalayas are the highest mountains in the world. They are between India and Tibet. Tibet is a region in southwest China.

Nepal and Bhutan are small countries in the Himalayas. Katmandu is the capital of Nepal. It is a historic city with many old temples.

Crowds visit the Hindu temple, being expanded at Katmandu (left). Farms thrive in the foothills of the Himalayas.

In Nepal, Mount Everest rises to 29,028 feet (or five and one-half miles)! It is the highest mountain in the world.

The snowcapped peaks attract mountain climbers

Mount Everest

and tourists to the
Himalayas. Only a few
people, though, have
climbed to the top of
Mount Everest.

Wild sheep and cattle

Argali (left) and yak (right)

live in the Himalayas. The
wild sheep of the
Himalayas is called the
Pamir argali. It is large
and has long, curled horns.

Wild yaks are relatives
of cattle. They are over
five feet tall and have
shaggy fur.

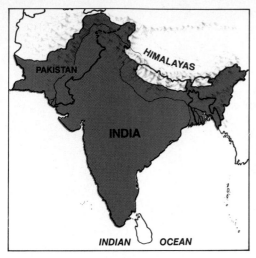

THE INDIAN SUBCONTINENT

Often, India and Pakistan together are called a subcontinent. A subcontinent is a large area that is part of an even larger continent.

The Indian subcontinent is a triangle-shaped peninsula. It is separated from the rest of Asia by the Himalayas.

Great Britain governed the subcontinent for ninety years. In 1947, India and Pakistan became free, separate countries. English is still one of the main languages in India and Pakistan.

Long before Great Britain, Arabs and Turks ruled the subcontinent. They built many buildings in the Muslim style.

The most beautiful of the buildings is the Taj Mahal.

Taj Mahal (left) and
Ganges River (above)

It is near New Delhi, the
capital of India. In 1653, a
Muslim ruler built the Taj
Mahal in honor of his wife.

In northern India, there is
good farmland near the
Ganges River. The Ganges
is the longest river on the
subcontinent.

Picking tea leaves (left) and growing rice

Farmers grow rice, tea, and jute. This plant is used to make rope and burlap bags. Jute is a very important crop in India.

The Arabian Sea lies to the west of the Indian subcontinent. The Bay of Bengal lies to the east.

Streets in Calcutta (left) and Bombay (right)

Calcutta is a large port in India on the Bay of Bengal. Bombay, a port on the west coast, is the largest city in India.

In most of the subcontinent, the climate is warm. Monsoons blow over the land. Monsoons are winds that change with the

Rice terraces in Sri Lanka

seasons. In India, summer monsoons are rainy, but winter monsoons are dry.

Sri Lanka is an island country southeast of India. It used to be called Ceylon. Sri Lanka exports tea and coconuts. Also, it is an oil-producing country.

31

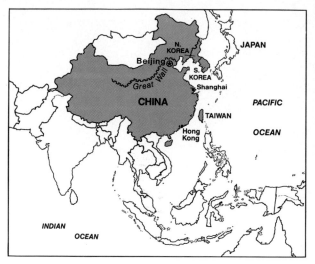

THE FAR EAST

The east part of Asia is often called the Far East. China, Japan, North Korea, South Korea, and Taiwan are in the Far East.

Much of China is in the central part of Asia. But because of many deserts and mountains, few people live there. Most Chinese

Great Wall of China

live in the east where
there is good farmland.

Beijing is the capital of
China. The Great Wall of
China begins near Peking.
It is 1,500 miles long. Over
hundreds of years, rulers
built the wall to keep out
enemies.

In 1271, Marco Polo traveled to China from Italy. He went overland, through the deserts of China. After Marco Polo, Europeans began to trade with China. The trip was long. But the tea, spices, and silk from the East were precious in Europe.

The largest city in China is Shanghai. It is a port on China's east coast.

Hong Kong is a large port six hundred miles

Hong Kong (above) and
giant panda (right)

south of Shanghai. It is a
center for trade between
East and West.

The central part of China
is the home of the giant
panda. The giant panda
looks like a bear, but it is
a relative of the raccoon.

Downtown Tokyo

Northeast of the China coast, four large islands form the main part of Japan. Honshu is the largest island. Many smaller islands are also part of Japan.

Tokyo is the capital of Japan. It is a port on the east coast of Honshu.

Near Tokyo, Mount Fuji rises to 12,388 feet.

A fast train connects Tokyo to Osaka. It makes the two-hundred-mile trip in ninety minutes! It is known as the bullet train.

Osaka is the third-largest city in Japan. In Osaka there are many beautiful temples that are over one thousand years old.

SOUTHEAST ASIA

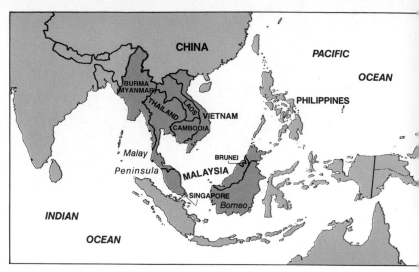

The countries of Southeast Asia are on peninsulas or islands.

Burma (Myanmar), Thailand, Vietnam, and Cambodia are south of China. Much rice grows in these countries. In fact, Burma is a world leader in growing rice.

Royal palace and Chao Phraya River in Bangkok, Thailand

South of Burma, the
Malay Peninsula juts out
into the Indian Ocean.
Malaysia is on this
peninsula and on a nearby
island called Borneo.

In Malaysia, the climate
is hot and rainy. Much of

Port at Singapore (above). The city is a
mixture of low buildings and modern skyscrapers.

Malaysia is a rain forest.
Rubber trees grow in the
rain forest. Malaysia
exports rubber to many
countries.

Just south of the Malay
Peninsula is the tiny island
country of Singapore. It is
an important trading and
shipping center.

Downtown Manila (left) and
a Moro fishing village on
Mindanao (above)

Indonesia and the
Philippines are countries
that are actually thousands
of volcanic islands. People
do not live on many of the
smaller islands.

The capital of the
Philippines is Manila, on
Luzon Island.

Jakarta,
Indonesia

In Indonesia, most of the cities are on the large islands of Java, Sumatra, and Borneo. Indonesia shares Borneo with Malaysia.

The capital of Indonesia is Jakarta. Jakarta is on Java, one of the most southern islands of Southeast Asia.

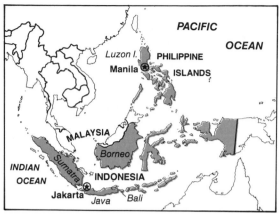

Bali Dancer

The volcanic islands of
the Philippines and
Indonesia are quite
beautiful. Bali, near Java, is
especially famous. There
are high mountains and
lush forests in Bali. The
people of Bali are great
artists and performers.

ASIA—FAR YET NEAR

The east coast of Asia is seven thousand miles across the Pacific from California. It is the same distance from western Europe.

When Marco Polo traveled to China from Italy, the trip took over two years! Now, East and West meet every day.

Ships load goods in the many ports of Asia. The goods are shipped all over

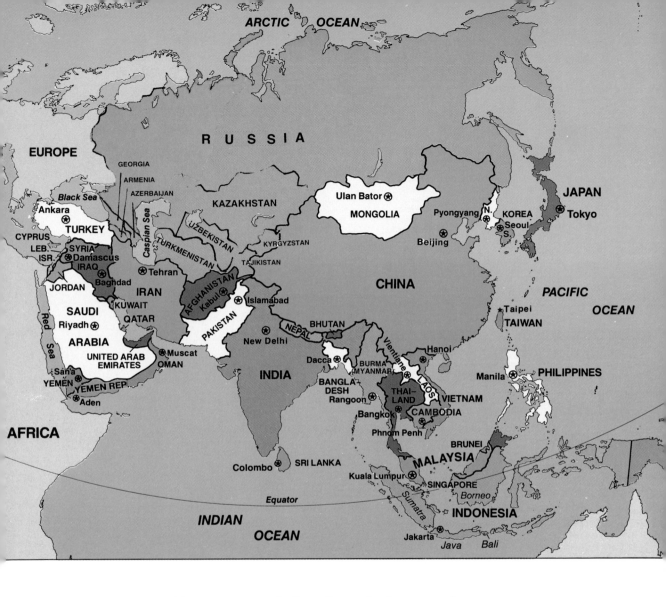

the world. And by plane,
Marco Polo's long trip
takes less than a day.

MAJOR COUNTRIES IN ASIA

Name	Capital	Name	Capital
Afghanistan	Kabul	Lebanon	Beirut
Armenia	Yerevan	Macao	Macao
Azerbaijan	Baku	Malaysia	Kuala Lumpur
Bahrain	Manama	Maldives	Male
Bangladesh	Dhaka	Mongolia	Ulan Bator
Bhutan	Thimphu	Nepal	Katmandu
Brunei	Bandar Seri Begawan	Oman	Muscat
Burma (Myanmar)	Rangoon	Pakistan	Islamabad
Cambodia	Phnom Penh	Philippines	Manila
China	Beijing	Qatar	Doha
Cyprus	Nicosia	Russia	Moscow
Georgia	Tibilisi	Saudi Arabia	Riyadh
Hong Kong	Victoria	Singapore	Singapore
India	New Delhi	Sri Lanka	Colombo
Indonesia	Jakarta	Syria	Damascus
Iran	Teheran	Taiwan	Taipei
Iraq	Baghdad	Tajikistan	Dushanbe
Israel	Jerusalem	Thailand	Bangkok
Japan	Tokyo	Turkey	Ankara
Jordan	Amman	Turkmenistan	Ashkhabad
Kazakhstan	Almaty	United Arab Emirates	Abu Dhabi
Korea, North	Pyongyang	Uzbekistan	Tashkent
Korea, South	Seoul	Vietnam	Hanoi
Kuwait	Kuwait	Yemen (Aden)	Aden
Kyrgyzstan	Bishkek	Yemen (Sana)	Sana
Laos	Vientiane		

WORDS YOU SHOULD KNOW

border(BOR • dir) — the outer part or boundary of something

burlap(BER • lap) — a rough, heavy cloth woven from jute

central(SEN • tril) — near the center or the middle

coast(KOHST) — land near an ocean or sea

historic(hiss • TOR • ik) — important because of the past history of a place

jute(JOOT) — a plant that is used to make rope

monsoon(mahn • SOON) — a wind that can be rainy or dry, depending on the season

nostrils(NOSS • trilz) — openings in the nose for breathing

peninsula(pen • IN • soo • la) — land that has water on three sides and is connected to a larger mass of land

port(PORT) — a city on a sea or river where ships dock

scroll(SKROLL) — something written on paper that is rolled up

steppe(STEP) — a plain where little rain falls and few trees grow

subcontinent (sub • KAHN • tih • nent)—a large area that is part
of a larger continent

temple (TEM • pil)—a place of worship for people of one religion

volcanic island (vol • KAN • ik EYE • land)—an island built up by
a volcano

INDEX

About the Author

D.V. Georges is a geophysicist in Houstan, Texas. Dr. Georges attended Rice University, earning a masters degree in chemistry in 1975 and a doctorate in geophysics in 1978.